❧ Hello Kitty's ❧
Book of Summertime Fun
by Kris Hirschmann

SCHOLASTIC INC.

New York Toronto London Auckland Sydney Mexico City New Delhi Hong Kong Buenos Aires

Cover Design by Carisa Swenson
Interior Design by Bethany Dixon

12 11 10 9 8 7 6 5 4 3 2 1   4 5 6 7 8 9/0

Printed in the U.S.A.
First printing, May 2004

SUMMER IS RED-HOT!

Hello Kitty loves summertime! The days are long, the nights are warm, and there's so much to do. Hello Kitty sometimes wonders how she can possibly fit so much fun into three short months. But she's going to try—and you're going to help! This book includes Hello Kitty's tried-and-tested summer fun ideas. You can do crafts, play water games, and make fun, tasty treats. You can even record your thoughts and activities so you'll remember them for next summer. With some help from Hello Kitty, you're about to have the best season ever!

My Summertime Goals

- A place I want to go: ....
- A skill I want to learn: ....
- A book I want to read: ....
- Something I want to make: ....
- A special activity I want to do: ....
- Other goals: ....

....

....

....

....

JUNE

TO-DO CHECKLIST

ARE YOU READY FOR JUNE?

Summer is finally here! All you really need to do is sit back and enjoy. But if you want to make the very most of your vacation, why not take a few simple steps to prepare? Here's Hello Kitty's checklist of summer essentials.

Hello Kitty's June Checklist

.... Gather some summer wardrobe items, like:

- ☆ A new swimsuit
- ☆ Sunglasses
- ☆ Flip-flops
- ☆ Tank tops
- ☆ Shorts
- ☆ Hats

.... Turn off your alarm clock! You won't need it for almost three months.

.... Pack away your schoolbooks and supplies. Hooray!

.... Find or buy a fan. It's going to be hot!

.... Hit the bookstore or library for summer reading material.

.... Buy some supplies at your local craft store. You never know when the creative bug might bite!

.... Tune up your bike so you can go, go, go!

.... Stock up on suntan lotion.

.... Buy a new water toy.

.... Get lots of batteries. You'll need them for boom boxes, flashlights, and other summer must-haves.

.... Get a local activity guide. Then ask your parents to help you plan a family outing. Mark it on your calendar now so you'll remember.

Other things I want to do in June: ....

....

CeLeBRate!

MIDSUMMER DAY

Midsummer Day is also called the summer solstice, or sometimes simply the first day of summer. It falls on June 21 or 22. (Check your calendar for this year's date.) Midsummer Day is special because it is the longest day of the year. The farther you live from the earth's equator, the longer the day will be. In some far northern regions, the sun never sets on Midsummer Day.

People everywhere celebrate the "official" arrival of summer. Here are some ways you and your friends can celebrate.

Wash your face with morning dew. Some people believe that midsummer dew is good for the skin.

Make a daisy-chain circlet. To make a daisy chain, pick a bunch of small summer flowers. Pinch a small hole in the stem of one flower. Poke the stem of another flower through the hole. Then pinch a hole in the new stem. Keep adding flowers until the chain is long enough to go around your head. Tie it closed with a small piece of thread. Wear your finished circlet as a summer crown.

Visit a farmer's market. Hello Kitty loves fresh summer fruits and veggies. Midsummer fruit—like strawberries, cherries, and peaches—is sure to be especially ripe, juicy, and delicious!

Tasty Treats

FREEZER FUN

Nothing is as satisfying as an ice-cold snack on a hot summer day. Hello Kitty loves these freeze-easy treats. They're simple to make and oh so good to eat!

⭐ **Frozen fruit.** For a quick snack, put a bunch of berries, cherries, or grapes into a zip-top freezer bag and freeze them solid. Then pop the frozen tidbits into your mouth. They're icy and delicious!

⭐ **Juice on ice.** Store a few juice boxes in the freezer. When you're in the mood for a chilly treat, use scissors to cut off the top of a box. Then scrape out the frozen juice with a spoon. Eat and enjoy!

✻ **Juice cubes.** Fill an ice-cube tray with different types of juice. Use the frozen juice cubes to cool your drinks. Combinations are fun! You could try raspberry cubes in lemonade, cranberry cubes in apple juice, or pineapple cubes in orange juice. Yum!

✻ **Cookie-cutter ice-cream treats.** Get some cookie cutters in fun summer shapes, like suns, butterflies, or flowers. Firmly press ice cream into the cookie cutters, then refreeze. When you need a cool-me-down, slide a butter knife along the inside of the cookie cutter to release the ice cream. Delicious!

Wet & Wild

Sunny Money

Trips to the movies or the mall cost money. Learn to earn! Hello Kitty can teach you some wet ways to raise cash for summer fun.

- **Offer your services as a plant waterer.** On the hottest summer days, who really feels like watering plants? You do, of course! Promise your neighbors that you'll take care of this chore in return for a small weekly fee.

- **Organize a car wash with your friends.** Gather buckets and sponges. You'll also need plenty of liquid car-washing soap. (You can find car soap at any grocery store. It's not expensive.) Make sure you have a hose nearby. Then put on your bathing suits, tape up some signs, and wait for the customers to roll up.

You can set a price or ask for donations, whichever you prefer. At the end of the day, split the profit among everyone who helped.

Go for a walk. You can also offer to keep your neighbors' dogs busy, especially during the dog days of summer. Determine a convenient schedule with a neighbor. Then take the dog for a walk around the block. If it's too hot, the dog may enjoy playing ball with you in a shady backyard. Your neighbors and their best friends will be happy, and you'll be in the money!

COOL crafts

SUMMERIZE YOUR HOME

Hello Kitty makes special crafts to welcome the summer. Here are some of her very favorite summer projects. Do them by yourself or invite a friend to help.

☆ **Paper butterflies.** Cut some pretty butterflies out of colorful paper. Use paint, markers, or crayons to decorate them however you like. Tape the finished butterflies to your bedroom windows. You could also use tape to attach pieces of thread to the butterflies, then hang them from your ceiling.

☆ **Wind chimes.** Gather ten objects that will clink when they strike one another. Hello Kitty has used old keys, seashells, and pennies, but you can probably think of other things. Tie, tape, or glue a 12-inch (25-cm) piece of string to each object. Then punch ten holes, evenly spaced, around the edge of a snap-on plastic coffee can lid. Tie the other ends of the strings through these holes so the objects hang below. Then punch a hole through the middle of the coffee can lid. Attach another string through this hole and hang your wind chimes where they will catch summer breezes.

Sun night-light. Cut a sun shape out of a piece of dark construction paper. Tape the construction paper over the light end of a flashlight. When you turn the flashlight on, you will see the sun shining—even at night!

keep in touch

care kits

At the very beginning of the summer, give any buddies who live far away or are going to sleep-away camp a special keep-in-touch "care kit." The care kit should include envelopes and postcards with your address already written on them, plus blank stationery sheets. You could even put stamps on the envelopes and postcards if you can afford it. Tell your friends they must use ALL of the items in the kit by the end of the summer—no excuses! Don't forget to promise you'll write back, too.

Other items I could put in my care kits: . . . .

. . . .

My Favorite Summer Things

On warm summer nights, I love to . . . .

When it's too hot to play outside, I like to . . . .

The best thing to do when it rains is . . . .

My favorite place to swim is . . . .

The best activity my family does every summer is . . . .

. . . .

Other favorite summer things: . . . .

. . . .

. . . .

. . . .

MY SUMMER DIARY

Use this page to draw or write about something you did in June.

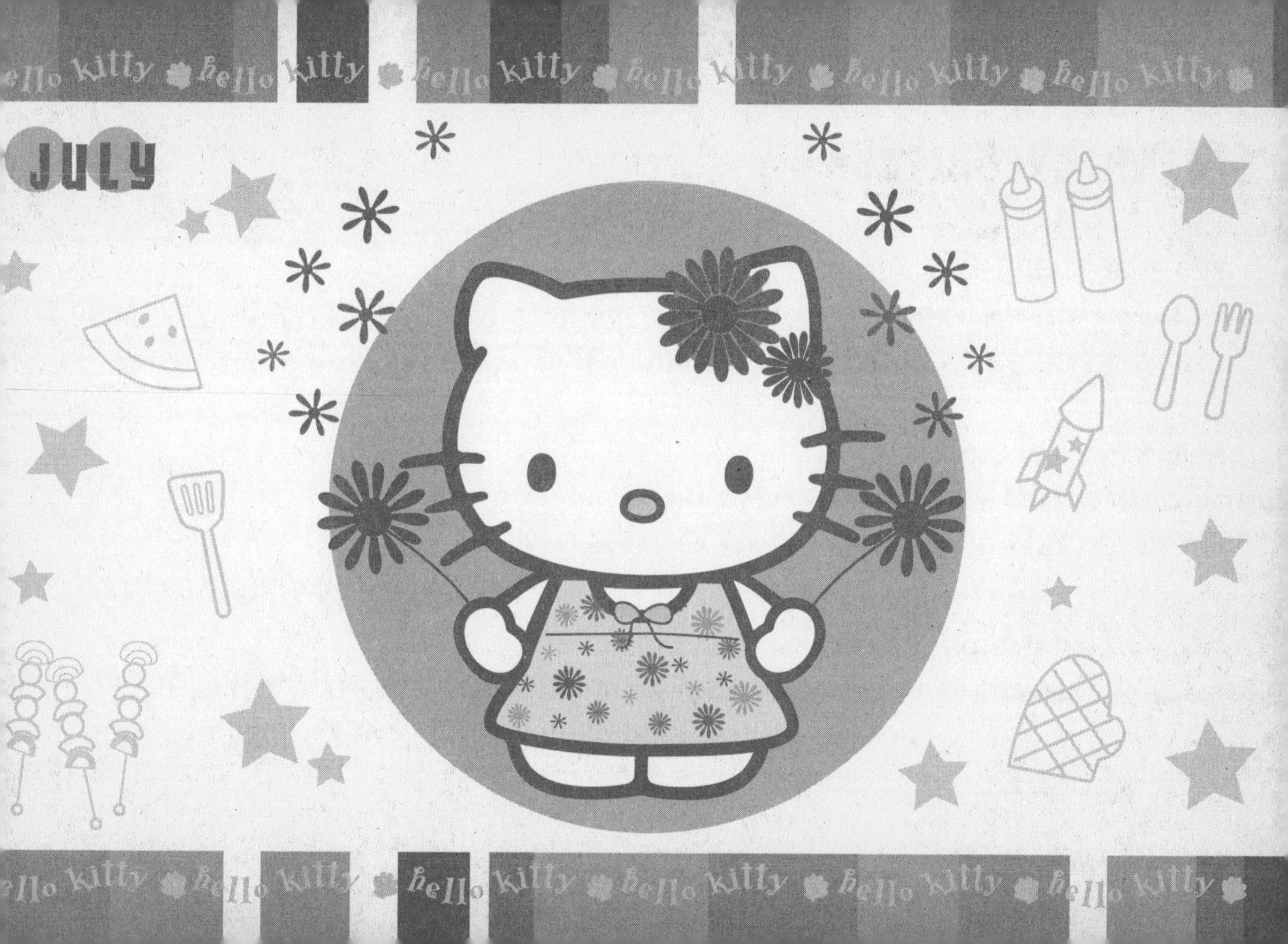
JULY
hello kitty

TO-DO CHECKLIST

are you ready for July?

Summer is almost halfway over! Have you been lazing the days away? If so, it's time to get busy. Don't miss out on Hello Kitty's essential summer activities.

Hello Kitty's July Checklist

.... Visit an arts-and-crafts show.

.... Take a trip to the beach or lakeshore.

.... Pick fresh fruits or veggies! It's fun to visit a pick-it-yourself farm.

.... Catch some fireflies.

.... Sleep out in your backyard or on your porch. Invite a friend.

.... Lie on your back and watch clouds. Decide what they look like.

.... Plan a sleepover or a pool party.

.... Have a squirt gun or water-balloon battle with your friends.

☑ .... Swing in a hammock while sipping a cool drink. ☑

.... Go for a nature hike.

.... Watch a movie at a drive-in theater (hard to find, but worth it!). ☑

.... Go fishing. If you don't know how to fish, ask someone to teach you.

.... Set up a lemonade or iced-tea stand.

☑ .... Go for a walk in the rain. Get soaked! ☑

.... Have a picnic with all your best buddies.

.... Gaze at the stars on a warm summer night.

.... Fly a kite.

Other things I want to do in July:.. ☑

....

☑ .... ☑

celebrate!

National Ice Cream Day

Every year, the third Sunday in July is celebrated as National Ice Cream Day. Did you know that about nine percent of the milk produced by American dairy farms is used to make ice cream? It's true! You can celebrate National Ice Cream Day with your friends. Here are some of Hello Kitty's favorite ways to remember this special and tasty day.

⭐ **Have a sundae party.** Get several different flavors of ice cream. Ask your guests to bring their favorite toppings. Spread everything out on a table and let everyone go ice-cream crazy!

⭐ **Ice-cream relay race.** Split players into two teams. Give each player an ice-cream cone or a cone-shaped paper cup. Each team also gets a Wiffle ball or another ball of similar size. The first player on each team places the ball on her cone. She must run to the end of the yard, turn around and come back, then transfer her ball to the next player's cone without touching it. One by one, the other players repeat the run. Which team will finish first? Remember, if any player drops the ball, she must return to the start line and begin again.

⭐ **Ice-cream craft.** Get a miniature clay pot (available at craft stores). Glue a large pom-pom or Styrofoam ball to the top of the pot. Use paint, glitter, or anything else you like to decorate your crafty ice-cream cone. This ice cream will never melt!

Tasty Treats

SUMMER SLUSHIES

When the weather is hot, nothing hits the spot like an ice-cold slushie. Hello Kitty loves pink, so she likes watermelon slushies the best. Mimmy prefers lemonade slushies. Both of these recipes make just enough for two drinks. (Ask an adult to help you with the blender.)

Hello Kitty's Watermelon Slushies

1. Cut 2 cups (480 ml) of watermelon into cubes. Take out all the seeds. Put the cubes in the freezer until they are frozen solid.

2. Put the frozen watermelon cubes, one 12-ounce can of cold lemon-lime soda, and 2 tablespoons (30 ml) of lime juice into a blender. Blend until smooth, then serve and enjoy!

Mimmy's Lemonade Slushies

1. Put 1 can (6 ounce) of frozen lemonade concentrate, $\frac{1}{2}$ cup (120 ml) of cold water, and 2 cups (480 ml) of crushed ice into a blender. Blend until smooth.

2. Pour into glasses and sip away!

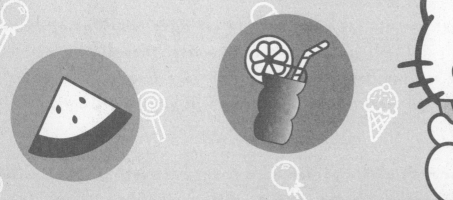

Wet & Wild

Water art

These activities combine two of Hello Kitty's favorite summertime things: art and getting wet. Try these projects for some cool and creative fun.

- **Water painting.** Ask your parents for permission to use a really BIG paintbrush (the kind you use to paint walls). Get a bucket of water. Then dip the paintbrush into the water and use it to paint designs on your driveway, sidewalks, or the side of your house. Work fast—the hot sun will quickly dry out your pictures.

- **Spray rainbows.** Set the nozzle on a garden hose to the mist setting. Stand with your back to the sun and turn on the hose. A pretty rainbow should appear in the mist! Hello Kitty experimented and found out that this activity works best in the late afternoon, when the sun is low in the sky.

Drip castles. When you're at the beach, put some sand into a bucket. Add water. Then scoop out a handful of wet sand. Let the sand dribble through your fingers into a pile. It will build up into cool-looking streams and drips. You can use this technique to build pointed spires. How big can you make your castle?

COOL Crafts

Fun With Fruit

Summer fruit isn't just for eating. You can also use it to make some amazing crafts. Here are some of Hello Kitty's favorite fruit projects.

☆ **Make a watermelon rattler.** Save the seeds when you eat watermelon. Spread the seeds on a paper plate and leave them in the sun to dry. When the seeds are completely dry, fold the paper plate in half and staple around the edges to hold it closed. Shake the plate—you've made a fun musical rattler! Use paint, markers, or anything else you'd like to decorate the outside of your rattler. Hello Kitty decorated hers to look like a big slice of watermelon.

✫ **Make fruit prints.** Cut a lemon or lime in half. Let it sit until the open end dries out. (This could take a few hours.) Then dip that end into paint. Gently press the painted fruit against a piece of paper. After you lift the fruit, its print remains. How cute!

✫ **Paint with blueberries and raspberries.** Use a spoon to squeeze the juice out of $\frac{1}{2}$ cup (120 ml) each of raspberries and blueberries. (Keep the juice in separate containers.) To each container, add $\frac{1}{2}$ teaspoon (2.5 ml) of vinegar and a pinch of salt. Stir well. Then grab a paintbrush and a blank piece of paper and get busy creating!

keep iN TOUCH

STORY-GO-ROUND

It's always fun to be creative. One creative way Hello Kitty keeps in touch with her friends during the summer is by writing a story through the mail. To do this, you'll need a small blank notebook. In the notebook, write the first page or two of a story—the crazier the better. Then mail the notebook to a friend. The friend should write a couple of pages, then mail the notebook to another friend. Keep the notebook traveling all summer long. At the end of the summer, get together with your writer friends and read the finished story.

My ideas for some fun stories: . . . .

. . . .

. . . .

My Favorite Summer Treats

The very best summer food is . . . .

The most refreshing summer drink is . . . .

The best candy to eat during the summer is . . . .

My favorite ice cream flavor is . . . .

My favorite summer fruits and veggies are . . . .

. . . .

Other summer treats I love: . . . .

. . . .

. . . .

. . . .

My Summer Diary

Use this page to draw or write about something you did in July.

August

TO-DO CHECKLIST

ARE YOU READY FOR AUGUST?

The summer is drawing to a close. You know what that means: SCHOOL! Yes, it's time to get ready to go back to school. Here are a few things Hello Kitty and her friends do each year to prepare.

Hello Kitty's August Checklist

.... Gather some school wardrobe essentials, like:

☆ Cool T-shirts   ☆ Accessories (belts, jewelry, scarves, etc.)

☆ Jeans   ☆ Jacket

☆ New shoes   ☆ Gym clothes

.... Get a haircut. If you feel adventurous, you could even try a whole new hairstyle.

.... If you haven't started it already, tackle your summer reading list.

☑ .... If you play an instrument, practice it. You don't want to be rusty when school starts.

.... Shop for school supplies.

.... Get a cool new backpack.

.... Stay up late and sleep in the next morning. Enjoy every minute. Soon you'll be up early every day.

.... Spend time outdoors every day before the cool fall weather arrives.

.... Make a photo album of your summer activities to show your friends at school.

.... Look through last year's yearbook. Read the notes everyone wrote.

.... Look forward to seeing all your friends again!

Other things I want to do in August: ....

....

CeLeBRaTe!

Family Fun Month

August is Family Fun Month. Spend some time with the people who love you and know you the best—your family. Here are a few of Hello Kitty's favorite things to do with her family during the summertime.

- **Spend the day in a canoe.** In the morning, work together with your family to pack a delicious lunch. Then head to a local lake or river and rent a canoe. Paddle slowly and quietly. If you look carefully, you can see all kinds of wildlife. Stop for lunch in a pretty swimming spot.

- **Head to an amusement park.** It wouldn't be summer without roller coasters, Tilt-A-Whirls, and other stomach-turning rides. How many times can you go on the biggest, scariest ride in the park?

🐚 **Go camping.** Camping is great for family togetherness. You also get to do all kinds of fun things, like cook over a campfire and tell stories in the dark. Hiking, fishing, and swimming are other cool parts of the camping experience.

🐚 **See a movie.** If you have only an afternoon to spare, why not head to the movie theater with the entire family? A dark, cool theater feels great on a hot summer afternoon. When the movie is over, grab an early dinner at your favorite pizza place. Talk about the movie you just saw. It's always fun to share opinions!

Tasty Treats

Summer Snowmen

Every now and then, Hello Kitty likes to bring some winter cool into her summer fun. Making summer snowmen is one of her favorite ways to do this. These juicy snacks capture the spirit of winter along with the great tastes of summer.

1. Gather lots of round fruits, like grapes, berries, cherries, scooped watermelon, and scooped cantaloupe. You can also use pineapple chunks.

2. Use toothpicks to stick the fruit together in the shape of snowmen.

3. Have a grown-up cut some apple slivers. Stick the slivers into the

snowmen's bodies to form arms and noses. (You might need to poke holes with a toothpick first to make the apple slivers go in without breaking.)

4. Use small tubes of colored frosting to add eyes, mouths, buttons, and anything else you like to your summer snowmen.

5. Eat and enjoy!

Tip from Hello Kitty:

You can also use marshmallows or gumdrops to make your snowmen bodies. It's not as summery, but it's just as yummy!

Wet & Wild

Games That Get Wet

When the summer heat is on, Hello Kitty and her friends like to cool down with water games. Do these activities outdoors, because you're guaranteed to get soaked!

⭐ **Ice-cube toss.** Grab an ice cube and stand facing a friend. (Make sure you're close to each other.) Toss the ice cube to your friend, and let the friend toss the cube back to you. Then both of you take one step backward. Toss the ice cube back and forth again. Continue stepping backward and tossing until one person drops the cube. The first person to drop the ice cube can make a special summer treat from this book for the winner.

⭐ **Sponge relay.** You will need two buckets, a sponge, and a bunch of friends. Fill one bucket with water and put the sponge in the bucket. Line up all your friends and place the other bucket (empty) at the end of the line. The goal is to get 2 inches (5 cm) of water into the empty bucket by passing the soaked sponge down the line. The last person squeezes the sponge into the bucket, then runs to the front of the line to start the process all over again. How long will it take you? If there are at least four people who play, divide into teams and race each other. Which bucket will fill up first?

⭐ **Fill the cup.** Any number of people can play this game. Give each person an identical cup, then turn on a lawn sprinkler. Each player's goal is to fill her cup with water. The first person to fill her cup wins the game.

COOL CRAFTS

SUMMER SAVERS

The summer is almost over. But your wonderful memories will linger all year long with the help of Hello Kitty's summer saver crafts.

🌀 **Capture summer in a jar.** Put something that smells like summer into a clean glass screw-top jar. Hello Kitty likes to use coconut-scented suntan lotion or an essential oil like mint. Seal the jar and use paint to decorate the outside however you like. During the winter, open your jar and take a whiff. The summer smells are sure to bring back memories of summers past.

🌀 **Make pressed-flower bookmarks.** Get two heavy boards. On one board, place a thick sheet of paper. Lay some pretty summer flowers on the paper, then place another thick sheet of paper on top of the flowers. Put the other board on top of the paper. Set something heavy, like a cinder block or a stack of books, on the top board. Let everything sit for a few weeks. Then take everything apart to get to your flowers. They should be flat, dry, and beautiful. Seal the dried flowers between two sheets of self-stick laminate (available at any office-supply store). Trim the laminate into a bookmark shape. Use your flowery bookmark all year long to remind you of summer days.

◉ **Make frost-proof flowers.** Cut out flower-shaped pieces of construction paper. Drip essential oils like lavender, jasmine, and lemongrass onto them to give them a summery scent. These fragrant flowers will cheer up your room on even the gloomiest winter days.

KEEP IN TOUCH

PICTURE POSTCARDS

You need to let your friends know about your fabulous summer. Hello Kitty updates her pals by sending her favorite pictures through the mail as postcards. To do this, get copies of photos you like. On the back side of any photo, write a note and your friend's address. Add a stamp in the upper right-hand corner. Then drop your picture postcard into the mail. Not only does your friend get a fun note, she also gets a photo showing what you've been up to. Send picture postcards to all your friends before the summer ends!

My favorite pictures from this summer are: . . . .

SUMMER HiGHLiGHTS

✦ The best thing I did this summer was . . . .
. . . .

✦ The funniest thing that happened was . . . .
. . . .

✦ These are the friends I spent most of my time with: . . . .
. . . .

✦ My proudest moment was . . . .
. . . .

✦ My most embarrassing moment was . . . .
. . . .

✦ Other things I want to remember: . . . .
. . . .

MY SUMMER DIARY

Use this page to draw or write about something you did in August.

AutogrApHs

Ask all your summer buddies to write notes on this page and the next. Keep these messages forever to remember all the fun you had this summer.

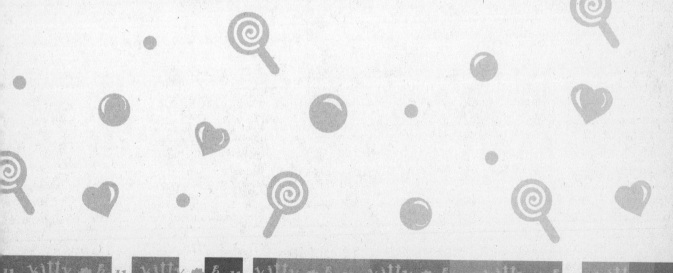